Disappearances

by Carol A. Fuchs

Published By
Capstone Press, Inc.
Mankato, Minnesota USA

Distributed By
CHILDRENS PRESS®
CHICAGO

CIP

LIBRARY OF CONGRESS CATALOGING IN PUBLICATION DATA

Fuchs, Carol A.

Disappearances / by Carol A. Fuchs.

p. cm. – (The Unexplained)

Summary: Explores the mysteries of the Bermuda Triangle, the kidnapping of a New Hampshire couple by a UFO, the lost colony of Roanoke, the Vikings in America, and the lost civilization of the Maya.

ISBN 1-56065-041-9:

1. Curiosities and wonders – Juvenile literature. [1. Curiosities and wonders.]

I. Title. II. Series.

AG243.F82 1989

001.9'4 – dc20 89-71351

CIP

AC

PHOTO CREDITS

Walter Aguiar: 6

Darryl Baird: 4, 11,

Gayle McBride: 46

U.S. Navy: 26

Virginia State Library and Archives: 18

CAPSTONE PRESS

Box 669, Mankato, MN 56001

Contents

Introduction 5
The Lost Civilization of the Mayas 7
The Lost Colony of Roanoke 13
The Vikings in America 19
Missing at Sea 25
The Devil's Sea 37
Kidnapped by a UFO 41
Glossary 47

Introduction

Have you ever lost something? A sock, or maybe a favorite T-shirt? Where did it go? How can it disappear? Most of the time we can find our things, but sometimes we cannot.

Socks and shirts are nothing compared to some of the big things that have vanished. There are areas in the ocean where planes and ships disappear without a trace. Even people have vanished. Early in America's history, a whole group of colonists vanished. Their leader left them, and when he returned, they were gone. Where did they go?

Years before the colonists vanished, a whole group in Mexico, the Maya, disappeared. We have records of the things they did, but no traces of where they went.

Around the same time as the Maya, we think a group of Vikings came to America. But where? Where did their colony go?

Today, we have more mysterious disappearances. A husband and wife from New Hampshire were driving along when they saw an odd light in the sky. A spaceship from outer space? They heard noises. The next thing they knew, two hours were gone. What happened in those two hours?

Many things cannot be explained.

The Lost Civilization of the Mayas

The Mayas were an ancient civilization. They thrived for nearly four thousand years. By 1697, the Mayan civilization was over. Many years before that, however, they built great stone cities in southern Mexico and the Yucatan (Yoo´-cah-tahn). In the early years, about 2000 B.C., they learned how to farm. From wild plants, they grew corn, potatoes, peanuts, tomatoes, and squash. They even used the stars to tell them about the seasons. By understanding the season, they could farm better.

By the time of their Golden Age – A.D. 800 – there were more than three million Mayas. They lived in the highlands, in the jungles, and on the coast. But by A.D. 900, the Mayas had all disappeared. All of the cities in the Yucatan were deserted.

Maybe some of the Mayas, moved to smaller, older coastal cities. Others may have founded new cities. Still others may have joined conquering tribes, like the Toltecs. Most were just gone. By the year 1017, however, the Mayan civilization was once again strong. Where were they for over one-hundred years? Did they disappear, from the face of the earth? Some scientists believe they did, but most have other answers.

City Life

Life was hard. Most of the land was dry. People had to work together to survive. A ruling class, called priests, gave everyone land and food. They stored the seeds for future harvests in secret places. The rulers wanted trade, so they hired crafts people, such as builders. They led a religion of many gods.

The Mayas did not have the wheel, yet they built great stone cities. They built pyramids taller than the highest trees. They paved roads out of stone. They invented a form of writing and created books. The Mayas made a great calendar and kept records of their history. Their sacred text was called the Popol Vuh (Pope´-ulvoo).

Water was very hard to find in the Yucatan. No rivers flowed there on the surface of the earth. Instead, rain water soaked into the land and formed underground rivers. The dirt was very soft in some places and caved in to form great holes. These holes filled with water to form wells. The Mayas called the wells cenotes (sen-oh´-tays). They built their cities around them. The cenotes alone gave the Mayas water.

Cenotes were important to the Mayas. Priests used them to give sacrifices to the gods. They threw the victims into the great wells to keep the gods happy.

Women walked barefoot to the wells with their children. They carried the water home in jugs balanced on their heads. At home, the water was used for cooking and drinking. The Mayas mixed drinking water with ground corn. The water looked milky. They called this drink posole (pho-soh´lay).

New cities grew. The Mayan culture grew. People grew selfish, however. One city would not help another. Cities fought each other. People had to struggle to stay alive.

Disappearance

In A.D. 890, something happened. Just what, no one really knows. One theory states that no rain fell, so crops died. Without crops, the people had no food. They starved. The fighting grew worse. The priests could not solve all these terrible problems. With no crops, the land soon eroded. People left the cities to search for food. The fighting became all-out war. Trade stopped, so there was no food at all. Major cities were abandoned. Other tribes, not Maya, came to escape their own drought. Thousands died. Then warriors invaded. By A.D. 900, the Golden Age was over. Mayan survivors ran away.

A few people believe the Mayas left Earth. They say many Mayan hieroglyphs (hy´-roh-glifs) show space travelers and vehicles. These people (who are not scientists) quote sections of the Popol Vuh and the Chilam Balam (Chee´-lahm Bal´-ahm), another important Mayan book, to make their case. They state: "Creatures arrived from the sky on flying ships…white gods who fly above the spheres and reach the stars." Does this mean that space travelers came to the Yucatan? Or angels? Most scientists doubt this.

In the 1950's, a discovery was made in Palenque (Pah-len´-kay), an important Mayan city. Alberto Ruz Lhuillier (Roos Loo-ee-yay) found the first tomb inside a Mayan pyramid. The tomb had a beautifully carved, heavy stone on top. The carving, Ruz says, shows an important man wearing a feather headdress. The man rests on a throne. A large cross with a two-headed snake is behind the man. On top of the cross sits a beautiful bird. At the edges of the stone, hieroglyphs show the sun, the moon, Venus and Polaris. Ruz thinks the man was a great priest. The giant cross represents maize (corn), a main source of food. The sun, moon, Venus and Polaris stand for the Mayan understanding of the seasons.

The people who believe that the Mayas escaped Earth with spaceships have a different way of looking at this. French journalists G. Tarade (Tar-ahd´) and A. Millou (Mee-yoo´) said, in 1966: "These hieroglyphs are certainly to do with the navigation of a ship. The man portrayed is wearing a helmet…his hands appear to be working levers; he has an inhaler in his nose…We find three 'receivers' for accumulating energy…The motor is in four parts…in the back a jet of flame is clearly visible."

Either explanation looks valid, based on the carvings

alone. However, Ruz, an archaeologist, knew about Mayan culture. He understood their beliefs and their religion. To Ruz and most other scientists, the drought caused many problems. Without food or water, people must leave or they will die. The spaceship theory only looks at the surface. It tries to explain the pictures without knowing anything about the people. Even if it had been possible to travel through space many years ago, where would the Mayas have gone? What did they do for more than a hundred years? And why did they return?

No one knows for sure what happened to the Mayas at the end of their Golden Age. They probably died from war, illness, drought and other natural disasters. Maybe they were invaded by conquering tribes, or they fled to other places. But they left no trace. Could the Mayas have left the Earth in a spaceship? Much like the Bermuda Triangle and the Devil's Sea, questions remain unanswered. Strange things happen. People do disappear.

The Lost Colony of Roanoke

Do you know who America's first European settlers were? Many people say the Pilgrims. The Pilgrims landed at Plymouth Rock in 1620. They were not the first European settlers in America, though. The first were French and Spanish, in the mid-1500's. They built settlements on what is now the southern Atlantic coast. This area goes from South Carolina through Florida.

In 1584, Sir Walter Raleigh (Rah´-lee) in England received Queen Elizabeth's permission to colonize North America. Raleigh felt that for England to be great, they needed a colony in America. He also felt he could get rich by starting a colony. A colony would provide new food and raw materials. Raleigh would bring these back to England and make money. Therefore, the colonists had to start farms known as plantations.

Raleigh sent two ships out from England. They landed on Roanoke Island, off of today's North Carolina, and then came back. The ships' captains said good things about the land.

In those days, the countries in Europe were often at war. Each country wanted to control the wilderness of North and South America. If an English ship came near a Spanish ship, for instance, the two ships might fight. The winner would take the loser's cargo. This was called privateering. It is a nice word for pirate.

Raleigh thought Roanoke was also a good spot for privateering. Spanish ships took treasures from Central and South America. The ships often stopped in Florida to get ready for the long trip home to Spain. With men on Roanoke Island, Raleigh thought his ships could easily attack the Spanish. Raleigh then sent another ship with men to live on Roanoke Island.

The men stayed less than a year. After they returned to England, Raleigh had a new idea. He would send families to live there. In 1587, Raleigh sent 117 men and women across the Atlantic to live on Roanoke Island.

After a month on Roanoke Island, the group's leader, John White, sailed back to England. Three years later, he returned to Roanoke. The colonists had vanished without a trace. Where did they go? Why did they leave? Their fate remains a mystery. We do, however, have some clues.

The Disappearance

When Raleigh's first settlers, all men, landed in Roanoke, they met the Native American Indians. Virtually all of

North America was inhabited by different Indian nations. It was their land.

The Native Americans near Roanoke were called Algonquians. They were primarily farmers. They grew corn, beans, pumpkins, and sunflowers. They also grew an interesting plant that the English came to like: tobacco.

The Algonquians dried the tobacco leaves and crushed them into powder. They took "the fume or smoke by sucking it through pipes of clay," wrote one early English explorer.

The Algonquians were peaceful people. The men Raleigh had sent, though, were soldiers. They had just come from war. All they really knew how to do was fight.

At first, the contacts with the native Americans were good. Raleigh's men, though, did not trust them. When one of the soldiers could not find a silver cup, he assumed the Algonquians took it. The soldiers burned the Algonquians town and their corn. The soldiers also used guns. The Algonquians had never seen guns before. The smoke and noise scared them and the gunshot wounds caused much suffering.

The English also brought European diseases to the new land. Smallpox and typhoid had been unknown. The Native Americans had no immunity from these terrible illnesses. Many became sick. The new diseases killed ninety percent of the Native Americans.

The English had to depend on their neighbors for food. The Algonquians were much better farmers. They knew the land. They knew which plants grew well. The Native Americans were able to survive in the wilderness. The English were helpless. All but fifteen of these soldiers returned to England. They had not liked the area at all.

The English families arrived the next year, in 1587. None of the fifteen men who had stayed were there. Where were they?

One man with the new group of people went away from the colony. His name was Howe. He was found murdered.

John White, the leader of the colonists, met with the Algonquians to tell them that the English came in peace. He wanted to start over with new friendships. The Algonquians said they would answer the colonists in a week. Soon, the Native Americans said they had killed Howe and the fifteen missing men.

White was angered to hear this. He wanted revenge. He and some men attacked the Algonquians. Only after the attack did they find they had killed mostly women and children. The colonists had said they wanted peace. Instead, they had killed. The Algonquians were furious.

Three ships had brought the 117 people to Roanoke. Two had already returned to England, and the third was about to go. The colonists worried about their safety. They needed weapons to protect themselves. They needed supplies. The colonists sent their leader, John White, to England to convince Raleigh to send more supplies.

White left on August 27, 1587. He arrived in England on November 8. Raleigh agreed to send seven or eight ships with supplies in the spring. When they were ready to leave, the Queen would not let the ships go. England was about to go to war with Spain. All ships might be needed for battle.

In April of 1588, White found a ship to take new colonists and supplies to Roanoke. They ran into some French ships though and a battle followed. Once again, White returned to England.

It was not until August, 1590 when White arrived in Roanoke. He found no one there. White found a sign on which was written the word "Croatoan." This made him think everyone went to Croatoan Island, farther south. White wanted to go to Croatoan Island right away but bad weather forced him to go back to England. He was never able to return.

Ten years later Raleigh sent another ship to Roanoke to

bring back wood and herbs and to look for the colonists. No traces were ever found.

Local legends in North Carolina say the colonists survived. They melted into the Algonquian population. The Lumbec Indians of Robeson County believe they are the descendants of those colonists. No one really knows.

The Vikings in America

The English ships that went to Roanoke were primitive compared to ships today. Raleigh's ships took two months or more to cross the Atlantic Ocean.

The English ships were like jet planes compared to the boats of the Vikings. The Vikings were warring seafarers from Norway, Sweden, and Denmark, 500 years before the settlers of Roanoke.

Even with their simple boats, the Vikings sailed far. Some people believe the Viking colony called Vinland was actually in America. This would mean the Vikings were the first Europeans to discover America, not Christopher Columbus. Other people question whether Vinland really existed. Was Vinland real? If so, what happened to it?

In the 8th Century, much of Europe was wilderness. People did not sail the seas. In fact, the Vikings were really the only Europeans who went to sea, which gave them great power.

Much of Europe was terrified of the Vikings. The Vikings could attack seemingly out of no-

where. Their boats were small, like long canoes and some had carved faces of fierce animals. Many of the Vikings wore metal or leather helmets and carried swords and colorful shields. With their surprise attacks, the Vikings would invade seaside towns. They took everything that was valuable and then sailed away.

It is no surprise that people who wrote about the attackers in those days considered the Vikings savage and evil. The Vikings, however, were not all cruel. Back home, they were farmers, hunters, fishermen, traders, and craftsmen. They had a written language called **runes**.

Few people were warriors. Most lived simple, average lives. Men hunted, farmed the land, and built the houses and roads. Women sewed clothing, cooked the food, and raised the children. Most of the warriors were just young men.

As the Vikings found new lands, they sometimes went home and returned with their families to settle. Some stayed in England and Ireland. Some went on to Iceland and Greenland. Some went to a place called Vinland.

The Viking people told stories during the long winters. Many of these stories, called **sagas**, were of adventure. The sagas were later written down.

Today, we can go back to these sagas to learn about the Vikings.

In ***Erik the Red's Saga*** and ***The Greenlanders' Saga***, we learn that Iceland, around the year 960, was fully settled. Many people lived there. New settlers found little land available. Erik the Red and his father arrived in Iceland from Norway. They had to live in a remote spot. Erik and his wife had a son, Leif Eriksson. (Leif is pronounced "life" or "leef." "Eriksson" means Erik's son.)

Erik and his family sailed west and found land. He called the land "Greenland" hoping such a nice name would bring more settlers. It did.

Around the year 990, when more people lived in Greenland, Leif Eriksson wanted to find new lands. With a crew of thirty-five, he sailed west. The first land he sighted had ice, rock and no grass. He sailed on. Some days later, he came to more land. The area had sandy shores and appeared flat and wooded. Still, he sailed on.

Leif and his group came to a river that went inland. They went up the river and it ended at a lake. There they anchored and stayed the winter. ***The Greenlanders' Saga*** says the group found plenty of salmon. The winter was mild and much shorter than those back home. They also found grapes growing and they could make wine.

Leif named the area Vinland, meaning "land of the grapes" or "wine land." In the spring, his crew loaded their ship with grapes. They arrived in Greenland and caused a stir with their grapes and stories of the mild winter. Leif's brother Thorvald and some others left right away to settle Vinland. Thorvald lived there two years until he was killed by a Native American Indian.

So what happened to Vinland? Remember that the sagas were told again and again before they were written down. The stories probably changed over time. For years, some scholars thought the Vinland story might have just been a made-up Viking adventure tale. Others believed, however, the Vikings would not have made up all of the details.

In June, 1961, Norwegian-born writer and explorer Helge Ingstad and his archaeologist wife, Anne Stine Ingstad, wanted to find Vinland. They explored a coastal area called L'Anse aux Meadows (lons oh med-ohs) in Newfoundland, Canada. They discovered a small settlement. The site had the remains of eight houses, a sauna bath, cooking pits, and a forge. Small objects such as a lamp, a pin, and iron rivets were also found. The objects were Viking made.

For the first time ever, this proved the Vikings had been west of Greenland. Was this Vinland? Or did Vikings go south to what is now the United States of America? L'Anse aux Meadows has few trees and no grapes. It does not look like the Vinland of the sagas.

Viking scholar Erik Wahlgren studied the old sagas in their original Icelandic language. He checked out many details carefully. In his book, ***The Vikings and America***, Wahlgren thinks he knows where Vinland was. There is only one spot that matches the details of the sagas. It is in Maine, just up Passamaquoddy (pass-uh-muh-kwod-ee) Bay, near the Canadian border.

What happened to Vinland, then? According to the sagas, the second group stayed in Vinland only two years. The group probably left behind very little. One thousand years can wash away a good many things. After Thorvald was killed, the Vikings did not want to live in such a scary place and they returned to Greenland.

Today, the search goes on for more Viking visits to North America. Archaeologists have found bits of smelted iron and copper in Canada, along with pieces of pottery. They think these items are Viking. That means the Vikings went further into Canada. Perhaps more things will be found in coming years to prove that Vinland was really part of North America.

Missing at Sea

"Calling tower," the pilot's voice crackled. "This is an emergency!"

The radio operator in the control tower looked at his watch. It was 3:15 p.m. Lieutenant Charles Taylor and five Navy bombers were in trouble.

"We are off course. We cannot see land...repeat...we cannot see land."

The control tower grew silent. The operator grabbed his microphone. "What is your position?"

"We are not sure of our position," Lieutenant Taylor replied. "We seem to be lost." Taylor had over 2,500 hours of flight time. What was happening?

The tower called back: "Assume bearing due west."

"We don't know which way is west," Taylor replied.

"Everything is wrong...strange...We cannot be sure of any direction...Even the ocean looks odd...

The radio operator told Taylor to fly north "with the sun on the portside (left)" until he reached Fort Lauderdale Naval Air Station. Anyone could find the sun, especially a good pilot like Taylor.

VW
02
VW
VW

Soon the radio crackled again. "We have just passed over a small island," said the pilot. "No other land in sight."

That was the last message Flight 19 sent to the radio tower. Five Navy bombers were lost. They had left Fort Lauderdale Naval Air Station for a routine training flight at 2:00 p.m., December 5, 1945.

Each plane had enough fuel to fly more than a thousand miles. The weather was sunny and mild. Pilots from other flights had not seen anything strange there.

So what happened? How could five Navy bombers and their crews just vanish?

A rescue plane, called a Martin Mariner Flying Boat, was sent out with a crew of thirteen. The radio tower received one message from the rescue plane—"Strong winds above 6,000 feet." That was it. The rescue plane, with its crew of thirteen, vanished as well.

The Bermuda Triangle

The search for the five bombers and the rescue plane covered 380,000 square miles of land and sea. Hundreds of boats and planes searched large areas of the Atlantic, the Caribbean, the Gulf of Mexico, the mainland of Florida, and many neighboring islands. Some of the boats were Aircraft carriers, destroyers, and submarines. They

searched the area for weeks. Nothing was ever found. No life rafts. No wreckage. Not even an oil slick. Oil from the engines should float on the surface, even if everything else had sunk.

None of the planes had made an "SOS," a call for emergency help. All the crews were trained for water landings. They knew how to leave the planes and use their life rafts. The rafts were located outside the planes. No life rafts were found. A Naval Board of Inquiry discovered nothing. "They vanished as if they had flown to Mars," one board member stated.

They had all disappeared in *The Bermuda Triangle.*

A Mysterious Zone

The Bermuda Triangle is in the western Atlantic Ocean. It covers an area from Bermuda in the north, south to southern Florida, west beyond Puerto Rico, and then back to Bermuda.

Since 1945, more than one hundred planes and ships have vanished in this area. More than one thousand human lives have been lost in it. No wreckage or bodies have ever been found. Sometimes, ships or boats have been found empty or abandoned. Their rigging and cargo are still there. There is no trace of passengers or crew, though. These empty ships are called "ghost ships."

The disappearance of the 5 Navy planes still continues to be a mystery. Why didn't they contact the base? The reasons will continue to make this a mysterious disappearance.

On January 29, 1948, a plane called the Star Tiger left the Azores for Bermuda. A crew of six, together with 25 passengers, flew that day. At 10:30 p.m., shortly before they were due to land, the Star Tiger radioed the airport tower: "Weather excellent. Expect to arrive on time." The plane never landed in Bermuda. No more messages were sent, not even an SOS. No wreckage at all was ever found. A Court of Inquiry concluded: "Will never know what happened."

On December 28, 1948, a DC-3 with 36 passengers and crew flew from San Juan, Puerto Rico to Miami. They sent this message: "We can see the lights of Miami now. All is well. Will stand by for landing instructions." They were never heard from again, and, once again, they left no trace. It was as if they had disappeared into thin air.

Between 1945 and 1965, 15 passenger planes disappeared. So did many military and private planes. Strange things have happened in the Bermuda Triangle for centuries.

On September 15, 1492, a captain's log mentioned a bolt of fire that shot across the sky and fell into the sea. Then, on October 11, 1492, the same log described a strange, glowing white water surrounding the ship. Days later, the ship's compass spun around. The first mate thought that the devil was nearby. The ship's name was the Santa Maria, and the captain was Christopher Columbus. His ship did not disappear, but the historic voyage to America was anything but ordinary.

In August, 1800, the U.S.S. Insurgent vanished with 340 men on board. Later that same month, the U.S.S. Pickering disappeared with a crew of 90 while sailing from Delaware to the West Indies.

On March 4, 1918, the U.S.S.Cyclops vanished with 309 men aboard. It was lost between Barbados and Norfolk, Virginia. The Cyclops was a 19,000 ton ship. The Navy says that this is one of their biggest mysteries.

A very odd case is one about an American schooner, the Ellen Austin. In 1881, west of the Azores, the Ellen Austin came across an abandoned schooner. The captain picked a crew to sail the ghost ship. Within hours, a violent storm came up. The Ellen Austin lost contact with the crew on the new boat. Two days later, they found the ghost ship. The entire crew was again missing. The captain still wanted to bring the mystery boat in, so he asked another crew to go on board. Another sudden storm attacked. Again, contact between the two boats was lost. When the second storm passed, both the ghost ship and the crew were missing. Three crews and one ship had vanished without a trace!

Many years later, on February 2, 1963, a 425-foot freighter named Marine Sulphur Queen, a very large ship, was on its way from Texas to Virginia with a crew of thirty-nine. It disappeared somewhere near Dry Tortugas in the Gulf of Mexico.

Where did the ship and the crew go? What happened to all the boats and planes that have disappeared in the Bermuda Triangle? Is there a good answer?

Ocean currents move very fast through the water. This could drag wreckage away from the Triangle and out of the search area. Then it would appear that all traces had vanished. The Gulf Stream flows north into the Atlantic at four knots per hour, but Coast Guard searches always cover areas far from what may be the wreck site.

Wrecked ships or planes that sink to the bottom of the ocean can be swallowed up by quicksand. A machine called a **magnetometer** can locate metal underwater, and even under the sand. Many relics have been found this way, including lost boats, planes, and even a train locomotive, miles from the nearest shore. What could a train locomotive be doing in the middle of the ocean?

Sometimes, things like bombs or mines from past wars can sink ships at sea. The wreckage, however, would float. Also, accidents at sea cannot explain the planes that disappear out of the air.

Another answer could be **blue holes**. Blue holes are caves and tunnels in underwater mountains. Sometimes these tunnels connect with lakes and ponds in the Bahamas. Once, a twenty-foot shark "appeared" in a quiet little pond more than twenty miles from shore. It had used underwater currents to go through the tunnels to the pond.

Very strong currents flow into the blue holes. This causes something called a **funnel effect**. A funnel effect makes a whirlpool on top of the ocean. Sometimes the whirlpools are strong enough to pull a small boat down into an underwater cave. However, even a large whirlpool could not drag down an entire ship, nor could it take a plane out of the air.

Waterspouts are another possible cause. They are tornadoes at sea. A funnel of water rises high into the sky and can easily tear apart a small boat or low-flying plane. Waterspouts can be seen during the day, so pilots can try to go around them. At night, however, they cannot be seen. At night they are very dangerous.

Another answer might be **tidal waves**. Tidal waves are caused by underwater earthquakes or volcanoes. They often happen without warning and can sink an anchored ship. They can break a large ship in half. A tidal wave may even bring back to the surface a boat that had sunk earlier. This could be the source of the "suddenly" abandoned ghost ships, but not with cargoes intact and belongings undisturbed!

Tidal waves will not pull a plane out of the sky. The skies have problems with wind, though. One problem is wind shear or CAT (for Clear Air Turbulence). If a plane flies into CAT, it can be like flying into a brick wall. CAT cannot be seen, but no one thinks that CAT made all the planes vanish in the Bermuda Triangle.

Winds and storms cause problems, both in the air and in the water. Hurricanes and typhoons sink many ships. Wreckage, or at least an oil slick, is almost never found.

What about problems with instruments and compasses? Some scientists believe that the earth's magnetic field might "act up" in the Triangle. Changes in magnetism create big navigation problems for ships and planes.

Other theories blame pilot error and running out of fuel. However, military and passenger planes have disappeared during normal flights. They have good pilots and modern instruments. They would not run out of fuel. Planes have vanished in groups. Could they have all hit clear air turbulence at the same time? It is unlikely. And why, with so many disappearances, has nothing ever been found?

Some scientists believe in space-time warps. These "holes" in the air or water are like invisible doorways to some other place. According to this theory, once you pass through this "doorway," you never return.

Others believe that the Bermuda Triangle may be used as a "collecting station" by beings from other planets. For one thing, the Bermuda Triangle has a very high number of UFO (unidentified flying object) sightings. Those who believe this theory feel that spaceships come to Earth regularly. These visits, they claim, cause magnetic disturbances. UFOs carry our boats, our planes, even our ships, aboard. Are these answers correct? There is no evidence for any of them. Too many strange things have happened to say any theory is wrong. Someday scientists may have an answer. For now we can only guess.

The Devil's Sea

The Bermuda Triangle is not the only place where things vanish. If you could travel straight through the center of the earth and come out on the other side of the world, you would end up in another ocean triangle. Here, in the Pacific Ocean, an area of mysterious disappearances is called the "Devil's Sea."

The Devil's Sea goes along the southeast coast of Japan, down to the northern tip of the Philippines, east to the island of Guam, and then back to Japan again. This area is larger than the Bermuda Triangle. Its size may explain its reputation.

Through the years, fishermen believed that demons and sea monsters lived under the ocean. That helped them explain why so many ships disappeared without a trace. From 1950-1954, nine ships disappeared with their crews. Like the Bermuda Triangle disappearances, nothing was ever found—no oil slick, no wreckage, no bodies.

In 1955, the Japanese government decided to find out what was happening. They helped pay for a research ship to study the area. They sent scientists to get information. The group's boat was called the Kaiyo Maru 5. They never returned, and no one was ever heard from again.

The Bermuda Triangle and the Devil's Sea share something else. They are the only two places on Earth where true north and magnetic north are the same thing. A compass will point to true north only in the Bermuda Triangle and the Devil's Sea. Everywhere else, a compass points to magnetic north.

The difference between true north and magnetic north is called "compass variation." While going around the world, compass variation will reach twenty degrees. At the Bermuda Triangle and at the Devil's Sea, there is no compass variation. This means that the Bermuda Triangle, true north and magnetic north all lie in a straight line pointing to the north pole.

The Devil's Sea also lies in a straight line with true north and magnetic north pointing to the north pole. In the Bermuda Triangle and the Devil's Sea, compass variation is zero. This may help explain why some captains or pilots get lost, or why some magnetic instruments spin wildly out of control. However, it cannot explain all the missing boats and planes in two completely different oceans, on two completely different sides of the world.

Kidnapped by a UFO

Inside the craft, the humanoids (beings who are not human) moved in a bluish light. The light cast no shadows. The creatures had very large heads. Their eyes seemed to curve around the sides of their foreheads. Their mouths looked like straight lines with no lips and no muscles. They had no noses, just two slits that may have been nostrils. Their skin was silvery, almost gray, metallic-looking.

On September 19, 1961, Betty and Barney Hill were driving home from Montreal, Canada, with their dachshund, Delsey. Barney thought they would arrive home in Portsmouth, New Hampshire, no later than 3:00 a.m. A little past 9:00 p.m., they crossed the border back into the United States. At 9:30, they stopped for something to eat. Soon they were on the road again.

As they drove through the White Mountains, Betty and Barney noticed an unusual "star" or "planet" south of Lancaster, New Hampshire. It seemed to follow them. Barney thought it might be a plane or helicopter, but it made no noise.

Betty looked through the binoculars. The thing in the sky looked like a plane without wings. It had blinking lights—red, yellow, green, blue. Barney was frightened. He and Betty kept driving.

As they approached Cannon Mountain, closer to their home, the thing seemed to float in the air. The colored lights changed to a white glow. Betty could see a row of windows. Barney left the car to get a closer look. The thing resembled a large, glowing pancake in the sky. He returned to the car and drove again. Near Indian Head, even closer to their home, they heard some "beeps." They felt tingly and drowsy. Then Betty and Barney heard more beeps. They kept driving, but still felt a bit odd. When they reached a sign that said "Concord—17 miles," they were fully awake. Awake, but different.

The sun was rising when they reached home. They should have arrived home by 3:00 a.m., in the dark of night. Betty and Barney looked at their watches. For some reason, both watches had stopped a bit after 11:00. They went inside and looked at the clock on the stove. It was after 5:00 a.m. They went to sleep.

When they awoke, Barney noticed the tops of his shoes were scuffed. Betty worried about radiation from the pancake thing they saw. Her sister told her a compass would measure radiation. Betty found a compass and went out to the car. The needle did not move until she reached the back end of the car. There, shiny, polished circles on the trunk made the needle jump. She did not know what the circles were.

Betty called Pease Air Force Base. Many UFO reports had been coming in. The next day, Major Paul Henderson of Pease AFB called for more information. He sent a report to "Project Blue Book," an Air Force project that studied UFO sightings.

On September 29, Betty started having nightmares. They lasted for five days.

On October 19, 1961, a scientist named Walter Webb talked to the Hills because they had spoken of space aliens. In the past, all these stories had been phony. Webb believed he could find the weak spots in the Hills' story. He could not.

Barney felt he was going crazy. He could not explain the missing hours. He also could not remember driving from Indian Head to Ashland (thirty-five miles). Betty also knew something must have happened to them during that time. The memory of her dreams still upset her. Barney and Betty both knew there was something they could not remember. Webb said this was called **amnesia** (am-nee´-zhuh). He told them to try medical hypnosis, or **hypnotherapy**. He knew it had worked well for combat soldiers who had "shell shock." Shell shock is a lasting trauma triggered by very loud noises. The Hills began hypnotherapy with Dr. Benjamin Simon of Boston in December, 1963.

Dr. Simon used something called time regression. With

time regression, the person under hypnosis goes through the event again. Dr. Simon and others say a person under deep hypnosis cannot lie. Dr. Simon treated Mr. and Mrs. Hill for more than six months. By the end of six months, both Barney and Betty seemed to remember the same thing.

Past Indian Head, Barney realized he had left Highway 3. He does not know why, but he remembers that he heard some "beeps." He saw a group of people in the road, and they all seemed dressed alike. The area was brightly lit, even though it was night. The people came up to the car and helped him out. He was very weak, but not afraid. Betty also remembers the people in the road, the brightness, and being taken from the car. Both remember hearing, "You will not be harmed."

As the men dragged Barney up a ramp, he scuffed his shoes. They placed him on a cold table. Barney said to himself: "I do not want to be operated on." The people studied him. Betty remembers going into a different room with an examining table. She was studied, too, especially her skin. Other people pulled at her teeth. Barney wore dentures, so the people probably wanted to see if all humans had teeth that came out. Betty's teeth were her own.

The beings guided Barney back to the car after the exam. Delsey, the dog, was asleep on the front seat. Betty came back. She and Barney watched as the "bright moon" left and went back into space. Barney felt happy. "There it goes," he said.

When they heard the next set of beeps, they had been driving for some time. They became more fully awake then and forgot everything about the UFO. The first beeps, near Indian Head, may have put them into a trance. The second beeps, near Ashland, woke them up. Their strange experience, however, was forgotten.

Did this really happen? Many scientists who have studied the case believe so. The Hills each described a strange event in almost the same words, even under deep hypnosis. Each remembered being taken aboard a UFO, yet neither knew what the other had seen.

The physical evidence is puzzling. What caused the shiny, polished circles on the trunk of the car? Why did the compass needle jump when placed near those circles? Why had both Barney's and Betty's watches stopped? What did happen to those missing hours?

Dr. Simon does not rule out abduction (being taken away). He believes that Betty's nightmares, which she wrote down and shared with Barney, may have put memories in their heads. They each believed they were taken aboard a UFO. Dr. Simon had no doubt that Betty and Barney were not lying on purpose. Yet no one was a witness to this disappearance.

The Hill case is ***the*** accepted case of alien visitation because of the visible changes. It is more believable than any other case. Not only that, many people have reported seeing these same aliens. Such sightings were the basis for ***Close Encounters of the Third Kind***. The aliens in this movie are exactly what the Hills saw.

Glossary

Amnesia: A loss of memory.

Blue Holes: Caves and tunnels in mountains under the water.

Funnel Effect: A whirlpool of water on top of the ocean

Hypnotherapy: Treatment using the practice of hypnosis in which the patient is put into a sleeplike state.

Magnetic north: The direction that a magnetic compass needle points to. This is not usually true north.

Magnetometer: An instrument used to locate items underwater.

Runes: Characters used to make up an alphabet used by the ancient Scandinavians.

Sagas: A story of adventures, heroic deeds, battles or customs told by the Scandinavians.

Tidal waves: A very large, destructive wave sent to shore by an earthquake or a very strong wind.

Waterspouts: A fast-moving funnel shaped column that extends from a storm cloud to a body of water.

DATE DUE
